# Cotswolds and South Midlands

## Michael Clemens

Ian Allan
PUBLISHING

*Front cover:* Collett 'Large Prairie' No 4100 waits for custom at Chipping Norton in 1962 with a train for Kingham. Passenger services on this line ceased later in the year, freight following suit in 1964.

*Back cover:* This colour-coded map is something of a rarity and was given to the author's father by the foreman at Worcester locomotive shed (85A) when closed for steam at the end of 1965. The colours tell railwaymen which types of locomotives are allowed on what route — and, perhaps more importantly, which are not. Despite being a GWR map it nevertheless shows most LMS routes.

*Previous page:* Viewed from the since dismantled Midland Railway bridge over the River Avon, a 'Hall' runs light-engine over the Great Western bridge into Evesham from Worcester. The picture dates from the summer of 1964, by which time the Midland line from Evesham to Ashchurch (closed the year before) had been lifted; however, a short section of track was left *in situ* on the bridge to allow access to the Midland freight yards from the Great Western side, until they too were taken out of use in 1967.

*Above:* A rare photograph of the author's father, seen in his element visiting Tyseley Motive Power Depot, Birmingham, with some of his pals on a foggy Sunday 25 November 1962. From left to right are David Evans (1924-), G. E. S. (Eric) Parker (1900-88) and C. N. 'Jim' Clemens (1922-87).

First published 2007

ISBN (10) 0 7110 3220 3
ISBN (13) 978 0 7110 3220 0

© Michael Clemens 2007

Published by Ian Allan Publishing

an imprint of Ian Allan Publishing Ltd, Hersham, Surrey, KT12 4RG
Printed in England by Ian Allan Printing Ltd, Hersham, Surrey, KT12 4RG

Code: 0705/B

Visit the Ian Allan Publishing website at www.ianallanpublishing.com

# INTRODUCTION

The Clemens family has lived in Pershore, Worcestershire, since early Victorian times. The town is situated by the River Avon in the Vale of Evesham, with the Cotswolds to the east, the Lickey Hills to the north and the Malvern Hills to the west, so not surprisingly there is extensive photographic coverage of our local South Midlands area. However, finding a title for this first book of photographs taken by my late father, Jim, and me that is both short and snappy plus descriptively correct has proved difficult. Primarily this book covers the counties of Gloucestershire, Herefordshire and Worcestershire but also ventures into Oxfordshire, Somerset, Warwickshire and Wiltshire; for the sake of completeness we even travel about a mile into Wales. Gloucestershire, Herefordshire and Worcestershire are linked by the Three Counties Agricultural Show and, perhaps more importantly for this book, by the Three Choirs Classical Music Festival, long associated with composer Sir Edward Elgar. In 1957, to celebrate the centenary of his birth, British Railways renamed 'Castle'-class express-passenger locomotive No 7005 in his honour. At the same time the premier express on the Hereford–Paddington route, serving the three counties on its way to London, became the 'Cathedrals Express'.

People regularly ask me if my late father realised at the time just what a priceless archive he was creating. Certainly he knew that, if he did not go out and film the various railway lines and the locomotives that worked over them, they would be gone forever, be it within a week, a month or a year. But what I am convinced he did not realise was the tremendous interest there would be decades later in old railways and nostalgia generally.

I have tried to select a mix of photographs that will appeal both to railway enthusiasts and to those with an interest in local history. Main lines covered, with both express passenger and heavy freight trains, include the Cotswold & Malvern line from Oxford to Worcester and Hereford, the Lickey Incline and the route south to Gloucester and Bath, the competing Great Western Railway (GWR) line from Stratford-upon-Avon to Cheltenham and that from Banbury to Hatton Bank. Those who enjoy rural tranquillity will appreciate seeing long-vanished railways, stations and trains at locations throughout the South Midlands, including Chipping Norton, the Stratford-on-Avon & Midland Junction Railway (SMJR), Stow-on-the-Wold, Fairford, Tetbury, the Golden Valley auto trains, Upton-on-Severn, Sharpness, Cinderford, Ross-on-Wye, Newent, Bromyard and Kington.

It would be impractical to list all the locomotive classes featured, but, as might be expected, Great Western types are in the majority, ranging from 'Kings', 'Castles', 'Halls', 'Granges' and '28xx' down through the 2-6-2 (Prairie) tanks and 0-6-0 pannier tanks to the delightful '14xx' 0-4-2Ts; there's even a 'Dukedog'. London, Midland & Scottish (LMS) representatives include

'Black Fives', 'Jubilees', an '8F', an S&D '7F', a 'Crab', Ivatt '43xxxs', Fowler '4MT' 2-6-4 tanks, MR '3F' 0-6-0s and a Stanier 0-4-4T. From the BR era we see '9Fs', a 'Britannia', '75xxx' and a '78xxx'. An 'A1' Pacific even puts in an appearance. Despite the title some diesels have crept in, notably 'Hymeks', a Class 14 0-6-0 and Brush Type 4s, plus the 'Blue Pullman', and AC railbus and a GWR railcar.

My father started taking black & white railway photographs before World War 2, and I joined in during the late 1950s; however the earliest still colour photographs date from 1961 and the earliest black & white in the book (a diesel shot) is from 1952. All the main pictures were taken by either my dad or me with a single exception, one by my mother. The colour films used were a mixture of Kodak Ektachrome, Kodachrome 2, Perutz and Agfa CT18. I am unsure about the early black & white films, but by 1958 Ilford HP3 was being used; by 1965 this had changed to Ilford FP3. The cameras I remember were initially a Super Baldina and later a Halina (although mostly used for black & white work); from 1966 a Minolta SR1 was used, which I still have (and it works). Some of the small thumbnail pictures are in fact taken direct from the 8mm ciné-film frames.

Regrettably the date and location of many of the colour photographs and the black & whites are not recorded. Establishing the locations has not been too much of a problem: they are all local, and I was often there at the time. However,

dates are more difficult and come from a multitude of sources; some I am reasonably confident about, others less so. For example, some of the Ektachrome and Kodachrome 2 slides have the month and year stamped on them by Kodak, some I can date from the ciné-film records, tickets or various railway magazines and journals. At the other extreme was one of our railway pals, Eric Parker of Worcester, who appears in the accompanying black & white photograph taken at Tyseley locomotive shed. Eric, who worked in the Worcestershire County Records Office, was a meticulous and prolific note-taker. His diaries for the last 40 or so years of his life were given to me by his daughter, Valerie, and if Eric was on the trip I can often find detail down to the minutiae. A favourite party trick of his for getting around engine sheds to collect the numbers was to take young Master Michael to the foreman's office. He would have been in his 60s at the time and would say something along the lines of "My 'grandson' would like to have a look round your shed; if I keep a close eye on him would it be OK?". It worked just about every time, and if anything he was keener than I was to get the numbers. Happy days.

The period from the late 1950s and through the 1960s was of course a time of tremendous change for railways all over Britain, witnessing both the elimination of the steam locomotive plus the closure of thousands of miles of track and stations. This is often referred to as 'the Beeching Axe'. Dr Richard Beeching was

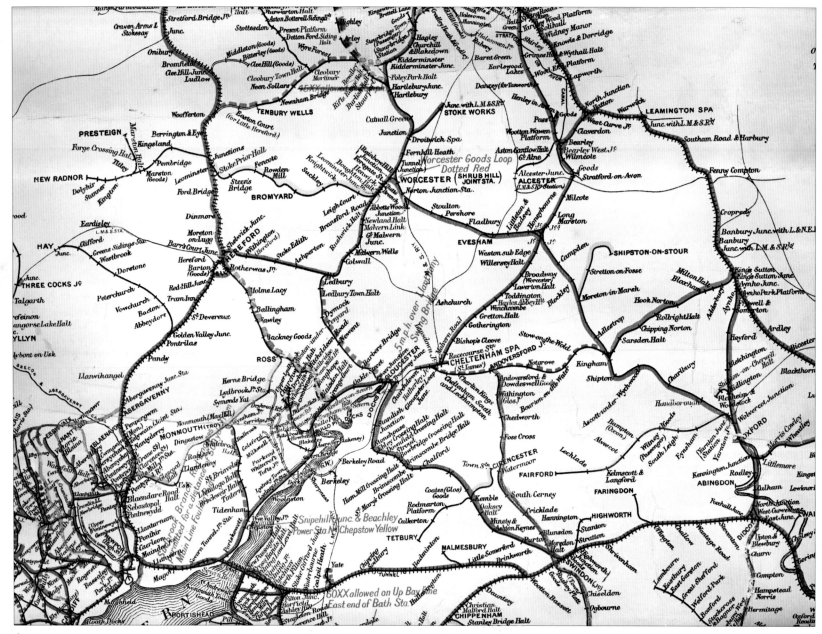

4

appointed Chairman of the newly formed British Railways Board in June 1961 by the Minister of Transport. His report *The Reshaping of British Railways* actually came out in March 1963, but, as you will discover from reading this book, a fair proportion of the network had already been closed by then. Over these years of great change my father built up a massive archive which, in addition to the thousands of both colour and black & white photographs, included miles and miles of mainly 8mm ciné film (thought to be the largest collection of its type in the country), reel-to-reel audio tape-recordings, tickets, books and general railway memorabilia. My father's day off work (Thursday) would often be spent in search of steam, as would (if work allowed) Saturday and perhaps even Sunday; equally family holidays would always have some sort of railway theme.

Looking back I think my mother must have been very tolerant! As long as it

*Left:* GWR locomotives were divided up into various axle load weight classifications, indicated by a coloured disc on the cab side. This colour-coded map is something of a rarity and was given to the author's father by the foreman at Worcester locomotive shed (85A) when closed for steam at the end of 1965. The colours tell railwaymen which types of locomotives are allowed on what route — and, perhaps more importantly, which are not. The area bounded by Halesowen, Bromsgrove and Redditch in the north, Fenny Compton, Banbury and Oxford in the east, Witney, Swindon, Tetbury and Bath in the south and the Forest of Dean, Hereford, Kington and Presteigne in the west represents the extremes covered in this book. Despite being a GWR map it nevertheless shows most LMS routes.

wasn't during school time I would generally be there, and I feel privileged to have witnessed so much first-hand before it vanished. But let there be no doubt: the credit for this book and the creation of the archive lies with my late father.

My father died suddenly of a heart attack at work in October 1987; afterwards my mother left the large cinema/music room (where all the films were kept) untouched until 1993. This room was cold and damp in winter but hot and sticky in summer, and unfortunately fungus damage has occurred to some of the colour slides as a result. Despite having been told a number of times that fungus damage does not affect Kodachrome 2 I am all too aware that it does, although Agfa seems to have been more susceptible. Happily the black & whites appear not to have been damaged at all, nor have the ciné films. The latter, although mainly Kodachrome 2, seem to have escaped through being wound tightly on a reel and thus being largely airtight. It was to try and repair fungus damage that I began experimenting with computer photographic programs. One of the problems with truisms is that they're not always true, and this is especially so nowadays of 'the camera never lies'. Most people will, I think, agree that certain photographic enhancements are legitimate, for example to compensate for deterioration through age of the original slides, to correct for wrong exposure settings or to 'repair' physical damage. However, there is a line between enhancement and fakery which I am confident has not been crossed.

Those who have read issues of *The Railway Magazine* from the 1930s and '40s may have come across the name F. W. Arthur. He lived in (I think) Fladbury, between Pershore and Evesham, and is credited with many railway photographs taken in the area. When he passed on my father contacted his widow about the photographs, only to be told that she didn't think they were of interest to anyone and had burned them. I was only a young lad at the time but recall that my dad was most upset that the archive had been lost. Sadly history partly repeated itself over the Clemens archive. When my mother was seriously ill the entire collection of stills, both colour and black & white, was dumped. Luckily my mother's gardener was most concerned and told me. I drove to the family house in Pershore, found the dumped pictures, put them all in the car and saved them for posterity; although after checking I discovered that I don't have all the black & white negatives. Sadly virtually all the entire paper archive, such as working timetables and signalbox registers, was burned. Fortunately the ciné films and the sound recordings were not dumped, and all survive. In recent years I have carried on where my father left off, holding film shows to railway societies and other interested groups, generally using the original movie films. Details of future shows can be found at www.michaelclemensrailways.co.uk.

*Michael Clemens*
*Pershore, Worcestershire*
*March 2007*

Wolvercot Junction, north of Oxford, is where the Cotswold line to Worcester (curving away to the left in this view) and the Banbury line diverge. Seen from the A40 road bridge on 5 September 1965, No 7029 *Clun Castle* passes *en route* from Banbury to Basingstoke with a Warwickshire Railway Society special. In total there were 171 'Castles', built (or rebuilt) from 1923 onwards, although not all were in service at any one time, the first withdrawal occurring before the final 10 examples had been completed. By the summer of 1965 *Clun Castle* (built in May 1950 at a cost of £11,640) was the sole survivor and was much in demand for special trains.

Having arrived from Oxford, '2251' 0-6-0 No 2221 pauses at Witney before departing west for Lechlade and Fairford on Saturday 16 June 1962, the last day of the passenger service. On the left, standing at the up platform, is a wagon being loaded with parcels from the Witney Blanket Co — as always seemed to be the case when the author visited! This station opened along with the extension to Fairford in 1873; the original station of 1862, nearer the town, then became the goods depot, remaining open as such until 2 November 1970.

*Left:* Fairford on Thursday 2 November 1961, and '2251' 0-6-0 No 2221 is about to depart (at 12.12pm) on the 25½-mile journey to Oxford. The GWR-pattern milepost by the signal indicates 89 miles from Paddington. The East Gloucestershire Railway had ambitions to create a through route from Cheltenham to Fairford and Witney, where it would join with the existing Witney Railway to provide a competitive route to London via the London & North Western Railway. However, objections from the GWR and financial difficulties conspired to ensure these proposals came to nothing, and the line terminated in a meadow a mile from Fairford.

*Above and inset:* The official closure date of Fairford to passenger and freight was Monday 18 June 1962. However, no trains ran on the Sunday, so this photograph taken on Saturday 16 June records the actual last day of service west of Witney on the Fairford branch. In front of the engine shed is No 2221, with a 'last day' chalking on its smokebox door proclaiming 'The Fairford Flyer'; not visible on the tender side is a gallows with Dr Beeching hanging at the end of a rope! In 1937 the locomotive shed here employed four drivers, four firemen and two cleaners.

Kingham (until 1909 known as Chipping Norton Junction) was a major interchange on the Cotswold line from Worcester to Oxford and London. Because of the poor direct service from Cheltenham to London it was often quicker to get the branch train via Bourton-on-the-Water to Kingham and then travel on to Paddington; indeed, in the down direction the GWR even operated a 'slip coach' service to Cheltenham from a non-stopping train. Kingham was also the junction for the Chipping Norton branch and, before 1951, the extension to Banbury. Both branch passenger services would cease soon after this 10 October 1962 shot of 'Large Prairie' No 4101 shunting its stock before continuing to Cheltenham.

No 4100 at Sarsden Halt with a train from Chipping Norton to Kingham in the summer of 1962. The line here opened in 1855, but Sarsden Halt did not open until 1906. As it served the village of Churchill one might have expected it to be called Churchill Halt, but it was named instead at the request of Earl Ducie, who leaved at nearby Sarsden House. Passenger services were withdrawn later in 1962, but freight would continue to use the line until September 1964. The GWR Third-class ticket (*inset*) was issued on 10 October 1962 — years after both the GWR and Third class had ceased to exist.

*Left:* William Bliss, of Bliss's Tweed Mills in Chipping Norton, was influential in bringing the railway to the town, at the time the second-largest in Oxfordshire. This is the second station at Chipping Norton and dates from 1887, when the extension to Banbury was opened, replacing the original 1855 station a little to the east. No 4100 was a Gloucester-allocated locomotive in 1962, when this photograph was taken, and would have worked across on the Cheltenham–Kingham branch. Latterly the weekday service between Chipping Norton and Kingham consisted of two passenger trains each way; passenger services ceased altogether in 1962, freight in 1964.

*Above:* Iron ore was an important source of traffic when the railway was extended from Chipping Norton to Banbury in 1887. The extension became freight-only in 1951, and following a never-cleared landslip at the southern end of Hook Norton Tunnel (*left*) the line ceased to be a through route from 1958. This shot of No 4101 from October 1962 might appear to show a train from Banbury leaving the east end of Chipping Norton tunnel and about to enter the station; however, the reality is that the Prairie tank has worked in from Kingham, run round its coaches, reversed them into the tunnel and is now drawing the train forward into Chipping Norton's down platform.

S 34276

LOAD 21 TONS DISTRIBUTED

By the summer of 1965 anyone wishing to see GWR-designed locomotives hauling long-distance expresses in the area on weekdays would head for Banbury. In this view 'Modified Hall' No 7904 *Fountains Hall*, tender stacked high with coal, has just backed onto the through York–Bournemouth express, which train it will work right through to its destination; 'Halls' continued to perform this duty until all had been withdrawn at the end of 1965. No 7904 had its moment of greatness on 15 September 1954, when, having replaced an ailing 'Castle' on the 'Bristolian' (the fastest Paddington-bound express of the time) at Little Somerford, *Fountains Hall* averaged 77¾mph between Swindon and London.

The last 'Castle' in BR service was No 7029 *Clun Castle*, withdrawn in December 1965 and purchased by Pat Whitehouse of 'Railway Roundabout' fame; however, despite being privately owned it continued in use on freight trains between Birmingham and Banbury. This photograph, taken on 21 July 1966, shows it at Banbury MPD (2D) in the company of 19 other locomotives — seven 'Black Fives', an Ivatt Class 2 Mogul, a pair of '8Fs' and nine '9Fs'. From here, in company with Pat Whitehouse and Eric Parker, the author enjoyed a footplate ride on No 7029 back to Fenny Compton, where his father picked them up.

*Left:* Stow-on-the-Wold on Wednesday 10 October 1962, with No 4101 leaving for Cheltenham with a train from Kingham. The station at Stow was about a mile south of the town, on the 475ft contour line. Trains started running through here from 1 March 1862, although the station was not completed until 1863. The last passenger trains ran three days after this photograph was taken, on Saturday 13 October. Freight traffic continued between Kingham and Bourton-on-the-Water until September 1964, so although the track in the loading dock looks rather rusty, the hand crane with wooden jib may have seen further use.

*Right:* In fading light at Notgrove, a last-day train hauled by 'Large Prairie' No 4161 heads for Cheltenham with a train from Kingham. All trains on Saturday 13 October 1962 were strengthened to four coaches, and the very last train of all, the 9.25pm from Kingham, had six. Some 760ft above sea level, Notgrove was once described as being the highest through station on the GWR, although this distinction was lost upon the latter's takeover in 1922 of the Brecon & Merthyr Railway, whose through station at Torpantau was at a height of 1,313ft.

Adlestrop station, between Moreton-in-Marsh and Kingham on the Cotswold line, was the subject of an evocative poem written in January 1915 by Edward Thomas. (He perished in the Great War, at Arras on 9 April 1917.) This photograph, taken on Sunday 4 November 1962, shows 'Modified Hall' No 7928 *Wolf Hall* bound for Paddington, having departed Moreton at 12.31pm. As a young lad in the early 1900s the author's grandfather was allowed into Pershore signalbox to talk to the signalman at Adlestrop, the furthest possible from Pershore at the time. The station closed at the beginning of 1966.

*Left:* Shipston-on-Stour became associated with railways very early on. The horse-drawn Stratford & Moreton Tramway, which opened on 5 September 1826, passed close by, and a connection was later built to Shipston. Subsequently, under the terms of an Act of Parliament passed in 1882, the tramway was upgraded, between Shipston and Moreton only, for steam-locomotive operation. In 1960 the author's father obtained permission, at a cost of 3/6, for a guard's-van trip over the by-now (since 1929) freight-only branch on Thursday 18 February behind BR Class 2 Mogul No 78001, which is here seen awaiting return from Shipston. Freight services finally ceased on 2 May 1960.

*Right:* The 4ft 0in-gauge horse-drawn Stratford & Moreton Tramway reached Shipston-on-Stour on 11 February 1836, and on 1 August 1853 a Mr Bull of the town's George Hotel commenced a twice-daily passenger service in each direction over the route. By 1889 the section from Shipston to Moreton had been converted into a 'proper' railway, but the route was winding and indirect; consequently the passenger service became victim to expanding bus services after World War 1, closing on 8 July 1929. Here an ex-GWR railcar visits Shipston (by now freight-only) as part of a Birmingham Locomotive Club tour on 24 May 1952.

*Left:* Aston Magna curve (50mph restriction), between Chipping Campden and Moreton-in-Marsh. No station existed here, although there used to be a siding and a signalbox. No 7027 *Thornbury Castle* was London-bound when photographed in the summer of 1963, by which time Cotswold-line expresses were the only ones to/from Paddington that were still exclusively steam-hauled. Withdrawn that December and sent to Woodham's scrapyard at Barry, South Wales, No 7027 survived the cutter's torch to be rescued years later for preservation.

*Above right:* The ascent of the Cotswolds scarp between Honeybourne and Chipping Campden involves a climb of about 4½ miles at 1 in 100, and a banking locomotive was kept at Honeybourne to assist (mainly) heavy freight trains. No 7031 *Cromwell's Castle* is seen about halfway up the bank. Great Western history was made here in the opposite direction on 31 July 1939, when the first properly authenticated 100mph in everyday service was attained by sister locomotive No 4086 *Builth Castle*, Driver Tidball of Worcester shed having been 'encouraged' to see what he could do by students from Oxford University.

*Right:* Honeybourne West Junction, and '9F' 2-10-0 No 92228 from Banbury shed is homeward-bound with empties from South Wales to the ironstone quarries of the East Midlands. The train is signalled for Stratford-upon-Avon, the other bracket of signals controlling the line to Honeybourne station and on to Evesham. The new yard complex just visible in the background (right) was opened in 1960, together with new junctions at Stratford-upon-Avon and Fenny Compton, in order to concentrate iron-ore traffic on the line through Winchcombe and Broadway, but within just a few years it was derelict, and the ore imported instead.

*Above:* Pebworth Halt was on the Stratford-upon-Avon branch of the Oxford, Worcester & Wolverhampton Railway from Honeybourne (opened 1859) but did not open until 1937, the GWR opening numerous such halts around its network to counter the loss of traffic to expanding bus services. To save on construction costs, railway sleepers were used, and passenger facilities kept fairly basic. Like many stations and halts on the old OWW lines in the area Pebworth Halt closed with effect from Monday 3 January 1966.

*Above:* A 'Castle' working hard northbound in very poor light at Pebworth Halt, with the author's father on the right. No record was kept at the time of the exact date or of which 'Castle' this was, although No 5000 *Launceston Castle* was observed on an earlier train, but it is amazing just what detailed researches have been carried out into locomotive operations during this era. Thanks to Michael Jennings it is possible to deduce, 40-plus years later, that the date was 15 August 1964, and the locomotive No 7024 *Powis Castle* (the only double-chimney 'Castle' with forward lubricator, Collett tender, bent handrails and no front number plate still running!), on the 12.10pm Penzance–Wolverhampton; apparently No 5000 had hauled the previous train.

*Left:* Gloucester Horton Road-allocated No 6947 *Helmingham Hall*, with what appears to be a non-standard 'home-made' smokebox numberplate, drifts south through Long Marston (between Stratford-upon-Avon and Honeybourne) in the summer of 1964. Built in December 1942 (and initially running unnamed), it later received one of the higher-temperature boilers, as fitted to the 'Modified Halls' built from 1944. Although Long Marston would close to passengers from the beginning of 1966 there would be considerable freight traffic to the Army base

*Right:* The 'Cornishman' was a restaurant-car express from Penzance to Birmingham Snow Hill and Wolverhampton (Low Level); it last ran on Friday 7 September 1962. Here 'Castle' No 5026 *Criccieth Castle* has just arrived at Stratford-upon-Avon from the south in the last few days of the service; visible below the train reporting code is the 84A shedplate of the locomotive's home depot, Wolverhampton Stafford Road. The waiting-time is being used to advantage by the fireman, who is in the tender shovelling coal forward for the testing climb up to Earlswood Lakes.

*Right:* The site of Aston Cantlow Halt in 1958; this was the view towards Alcester on the line from Bearley, a branch with a different history from most. Opened in 1876, it was closed on 1 January 1917, the rails being removed for wartime purposes. It was re-laid after the war, and Aston Cantlow Halt opened in 1922. Passenger services on the branch ceased again on 25 September 1939, although a 1949 timetable states 'service suspended'. The line was retained as a siding, often for wagon storage, until February 1960.

*Above:* The most powerful locomotives in the GWR fleet were the 'King' 4-6-0s. Here No 6005 *King George II* climbs Hatton Bank, between Leamington Spa and Birmingham (Snow Hill), in the summer of 1962; the third track (on the right) was for slower freight trains. Having suffered a collapse some years earlier the bridge had had to be rebuilt, as is evident from the new brickwork on the far side. All 30 'Kings' would be taken out of service by the end of the year, although three survive in preservation.

*Right:* Ascending Hatton Bank, west of Warwick, on 29 September 1962 with a down express freight is No 6991 *Acton Burnell Hall*, a member of the 'Modified Hall' class. In total there were 330 'Halls', of which the last 71, built between 1944 and 1950, were of the 'modified' variety; these had continuous frames and bolt-on cylinders with a separate smokebox saddle. The Standard No 1 boiler was also altered to give a higher steam temperature, about 580°F instead of 530°F. This excellent boiler was used on a number of different GWR classes, more than 1,000 being constructed from 1903 to 1961.

The evening 'Birmingham Pullman' from Paddington passes Fenny Compton, between Banbury and Leamington Spa, in the summer of 1962. Interestingly contemporary Ian Allan 'ABCs' describe the 'Blue Pullman' units as having 425hp motors, which always seemed rather high; recent research has revealed that the 425 relates to amps (A) and not horsepower! To the right is the Stratford-upon-Avon & Midland Junction (SMJ) line, by this time freight-only, being used particularly for iron-ore trains bound for South Wales; a new junction installed here only two years earlier permitted through running of these trains from Banbury.

*Left:* One of the most obscure railways in the country was the Edge Hill Light Railway (near Banbury), constructed under the terms of the Light Railway Acts to tap local iron-ore deposits, output commencing late in 1922. This 1958 photograph shows the top of the rope-worked incline that raised the railway 300ft up a gradient of 1 in 6. The quarries had a productive life of barely two years, and the last load made its way down the incline on 27 January 1925. Instead of being sold for scrap everything just slowly rusted away; the locomotives even survived World War 2, being finally cut up in 1946, while the company itself was not wound up until 1957.

*Below:* On 24 April 1965 the Stephenson Locomotive Society ran a last train over the Stratford-upon-Avon & Midland Junction line. Here ex-LMS '4F' 0-6-0 No 44188 hauls the train eastbound up the formidable obstacle of Goldicote Cutting, between Stratford-upon-Avon and Ettington. The cutting, 60ft deep and on a gradient of 1 in 80, was one of the few parts of the SMJ not engineered for double track. A nature reserve since 1987, its attractions now include spotted and bee orchids, plus the common lizard.

Two views of Stratford-on-Avon Old Town (SMJR). The panoramic shot of the station area and locomotive shed was taken during the 'South Midlander' railtour of 24 April 1955; the locomotive is 'Dukedog' 4-4-0 No 9015, the strange name being derived from the fact that they were assembled (in the late 1930s) with parts from existing 'Duke' and 'Bulldog' locomotives. Passenger services here finished on 7 April 1952, the shed closing on 22 July 1957, but freight continued until 1965. The second picture records the view west in 1958, with the line to Broom Junction on the left and the connection to the GWR on the right.

SPECIAL TRIP-3rd
APRIL 24th, 1955
RAILWAY ENTHUSIASTS CLUB
"THE SOUTH MIDLANDER"
Oxford to Kingham, Chipping Norton,
Adderbury, Banbury South, Fenny Compton
(L.M.), Stratford-upon-Avon, Broom Jct.
Evesham, Moreton-in-Marsh, Shipston-on-
Stour, Kingham, Yarnton and Oxford.
(W)       For Conditions see over

056    056

*Right:* The view south from the road bridge by Toddington station, nowadays the headquarters of the Gloucestershire–Warwickshire Railway. The date was November 1966, by which time the station had been closed and the local Cheltenham–Honeybourne service withdrawn for more than six years. The train, headed by a Brush Type 4 diesel, was typical fare for the line in its final years, being a Sunday diversion necessitated by engineering work on the ex-LMS line north of Cheltenham through Ashchurch.

*Right:* It used to be said that 'GWR' stood for 'Great Way Round', because in the early days many of its lines were routed indirectly between major centres, *e.g.* from London to Birmingham via Oxford; another example was that from Gloucester to Birmingham via Newent, Ledbury, Worcester and Kidderminster. In the early 1900s the GWR addressed the situation by building a number of new lines, including one between Gloucester and Birmingham via Stratford. By the late 1960s, however, the 'new' line saw little traffic; this long freight, seen heading south at Bishop's Cleeve behind Brush Type 4 diesel-electric No D1743, was diverted because of Sunday engineering work on the ex-LMS route through Ashchurch.

*Right:* The view south from the B4077 road bridge by Toddington station, on the ex-GWR route between Stratford-upon-Avon and Cheltenham, on a dismal day in November 1979, just after the track had been lifted. Toddington is nowadays the headquarters of the Gloucestershire–Warwickshire Railway and presents a very different scene: since 1981 volunteers have restored the station buildings and platforms and more than 10 miles of line, as well as locomotives (steam and diesel) and rolling stock.

Adding to the already impressive total of stations around the town, another, Cheltenham Racecourse, was opened by the GWR in 1912, on the recently opened direct line to the north; it dealt mainly with race-meeting traffic. On Gold Cup day (21 March) 1968 'Hymek' Type 3 diesel-hydraulic No D7080 has charge of a nine-coach train for Newport and Cardiff. At the opposite platform can be seen the rear coach of the 17.50 departure for Wolverhampton, hauled by Brush Type 4 diesel-electric No D1725. Still in the booking office, although by now seven years out of date, was a Cheltenham (Western Region) departure board *(left)*. Closed completely in the 1970s, the station nowadays sees trains again as the southern terminus of the Gloucestershire–Warwickshire Railway.

*Right:* Cheltenham Malvern Road station on Saturday 1 January 1966 (the weekend it closed), with a Nash Metropolitan parked outside. Malvern Road was opened in 1906 for services on the GWR's new direct route from Gloucester to Birmingham, it being impractical for these to use the existing terminus of St James. Cheltenham must have been a very expensive place for the railways, as at one time the town had seven separate stations open for custom; paradoxically it has always suffered from a very poor direct service to London.

*Left:* By the summer of 1965 there were virtually no steam-hauled express passenger services left in Gloucestershire, Herefordshire and Worcestershire. Exceptions were the Saturday holidaymakers' trains from the Birmingham area to West Country resorts, steam-hauled as far as Bristol. Three 'Britannia' Pacifics were transferred to Wolverhampton (Oxley) specifically for these services. On a dismal summer's evening No 70045 *Lord Rowallan* waits to head north from Cheltenham (Malvern Road) on a return working, with the closed engine shed behind. The 'Britannias' would be the final express-passenger locomotives to remain in service nationally, No 70045 hauling its last (coal) train, from Burnley to Wigan, on 1 January 1968.

The line between Honeybourne and Evesham was opened in 1853 by the Oxford, Worcester & Wolverhampton Railway, but Littleton & Badsey station did not open until 1885. Because of the level crossing here the signalbox was open continuously, but this was replaced by a ground frame from 20 September 1971, when the track between Evesham and Moreton-in-Marsh was singled; the station at Littleton & Badsey closed a few days after this photograph was taken on Boxing Day 1965. An interesting piece of railway trivia, related in the March 1946 issue of *Railways*, is the fact that between here and Kingham (a distance of just under 20 miles) the railway crossed no fewer than 12 county boundaries — surely a record.

*Left:* The view towards Worcester from the passenger footbridge at Evesham station on 5 November 1962. This stretch of the Oxford, Worcester & Wolverhampton Railway had been opened in 1852, the section east to Moreton-in-Marsh following a year later. The author recalls during the severe winter of 1962/3 standing on this bridge and trying to throw snowballs down locomotive chimneys! At this time agricultural produce from the Vale of Evesham was still being shipped by rail, but the track through the goods shed (left) was taken out of use in March 1966.

*Below:* The evening Worcester–London express arrives at Evesham during the spring of 1964 in the capable hands of 'Modified Hall' No 6960 *Raveningham Hall* (since preserved). This photograph was taken from the 'Black Bridges' that extended over both the GW and LMS tracks. Curving away to the left in the distance is the line to Ashchurch, which closed in 1963; close by it is Evesham GW locomotive shed (with its conical water tower), which closed in June 1961. Regular steam haulage of the London trains ceased in 1963, so this was a substitution for a failed diesel — quite common from autumn 1963 through to spring 1964.

*Right:* One of the few photographs taken by the author's mother. A summer's evening in 1963, and 'Castle' No 7005 *Sir Edward Elgar* is homeward-bound between Evesham and Worcester on the down 'Cathedrals Express' from London. There was a long-term severe speed restriction here on the bridge over the River Avon, a little to the east of Fladbury station. No 7005 is still travelling slowly but accelerating powerfully — very good for the tape recordings being made. Note the sign 'requesting' that passengers cross the tracks by means of the bridge, to which reference is made opposite.

*Right:* From 1962 the author travelled regularly through Fladbury on the train from Pershore to school at Evesham. This was the scene of a tragic accident, when a schoolboy using the flat barrow crossing rather than the road overbridge was hit by an express and killed. Attention was drawn to the fact that the warning notice (see opposite page) merely 'requested' that passengers use the bridge. The new metal barrier visible at the foot of the picture was fitted as a result. Photographed on Boxing Day 1965, a Brush Type 4 heads for Evesham. Like many of the stations on the Cotswold line, Fladbury closed on 3 January 1966.

*Right:* A specially cleaned No 7023 *Penrice Castle* hauled the final scheduled steam-hauled Worcester–Paddington express, at the end of the summer timetable on Saturday 7 September 1963. Departure from Worcester (Shrub Hill) was at 11.10am, and here No 7023 is pulling away from the long-term speed restriction over the Avon bridge at Fladbury prior to making its first stop at Evesham. The bridge was finally replaced between 10 and 11 November 1963.

35

The end of 1965 was a traumatic time for the Cotswold line: steam was coming to an end, and many of the smaller stations and halts were faced with imminent closure. On a cold and sunny Boxing Day the author and his father visited many of these for one last time. This was the view west at Wyre Halt, between Worcester and Evesham, with the B4084 road bridge crossing the line on the skew. Cheaply constructed in an effort to win back passengers from the buses, the halt had opened in 1934 to serve the village of Wyre Piddle; tickets could be purchased from a private dwelling in Chapel Lane.

Pershore in May 1969. When the author started travelling from here to school at Evesham in 1962 there were healthy passenger and freight services, but the following years saw the closure of all the nearby halts and stations, the withdrawal of the freight service and, in 1971, the singling of the track; eventually Pershore was served by just one stopping train in each direction. Thanks in part to the Cotswold Line Promotion Group things are nowadays very different: for most of the day the passenger service on the single track has increased to such an extent that no more trains can be run — and at the time of writing (March 2007) consideration was being given to re-doubling the line. How things change.

*Right:* In 1957, to mark the centenary of the great composer's birth, No 7005 *Lamphey Castle* was renamed *Sir Edward Elgar*, and the 'Cathedrals Express' was inaugurated between Worcester and Paddington. On a wet Saturday 7 September 1963 the same locomotive, albeit in poor condition externally, was provided for the last scheduled steam working of this train from Worcester, being seen here waiting to take over at Shrub Hill station; the constituent portions of this train originated from Kidderminster and Hereford, the former arriving behind a Prairie tank, the latter No 7027 *Thornbury Castle*. No 7005's career would draw to a close a year later, in September 1964.

*Left:* The residents of Worcester were sidelined by the Birmingham & Gloucester Railway (B&G), whose line bypassed the city when it opened in 1840. Worcester eventually got its station in 1850, when the Oxford, Worcester & Wolverhampton Railway built a line into the city from the B&G at Abbotswood Junction, near Norton. Here, in the summer of 1963 — shortly before 'Hymek' diesel-hydraulics took over — 'Castle' No 7005 *Sir Edward Elgar* prepares to leave Shrub Hill for Paddington. This locomotive was built in June 1946 and by the end of 1963 had covered 869,370 miles.

Pannier tank No 3682 in the goods depot at Worcester shed (85A) on Sunday 28 November 1965. This locomotive would survive to the end of steam here on 31 December 1965, being noted on that day with the chalking 'Best of the Last' whilst towing away already-withdrawn No 6876 *Kingsland Grange*. The author's father, through his directorship from the late 1950s of Worcester City Football Club (which team beat Liverpool 2-1 in the 1959 FA Cup), met fellow director Gordon Richards, who was a foreman at Worcester shed; over the years their friendship brought many benefits, not least the map that appears in the Introduction to this book.

Class A1 Pacific No 60114 *W. P. Allen* was not a locomotive one would expect to see on shed at Worcester, being more at home hauling crack expresses on the East Coast main line, but on 12 July 1964 it was the chosen motive power for the first leg of a Derbyshire Railway Society special to South Wales. It seems a Worcester driver, anxious to try out this stranger, generated such violent slipping in the shed yard that it seriously damaged the motion, and the locomotive was unceremoniously shunted out of the way pending the arrival of replacement parts.

The Western Region aimed for complete elimination of steam by the end of 1965 and duly achieved this, becoming the first BR region to do so. This was the scene at Worcester shed on Thursday 28 October 1965, two months before the end. Prairie tank No 6147, with a blue disc (just beneath the cabside numberplate) indicating its route availability, looks commendably clean in the circumstances; built in 1933, it would survive until December. Behind, also with a blue disc, is double-chimney '9F' 2-10-0 No 92235, built at Crewe in 1958 and destined to be withdrawn from Bristol Barrow Road shed (82E) in November.

Worcester locomotive shed was always one of the most difficult to get around, but, by way of compensation, the adjacent high ground afforded a lovely panoramic view. This shot, taken during the 1955 railway strike, shows the passenger depot in the middle and the goods depot to the right. Worcester was notable for being one of only two GWR sheds with a mechanical coaling system (to the right of the water tank); most relied on extensive manual handling, on account of the friable nature of Welsh steam coal.

*Right:* The view south at Halesowen in the early 1960s, with '57xx' 0-6-0PT No 3658, allocated to Stourbridge depot (84F), standing by the signalbox. The branch from Old Hill through Halesowen and on to Longbridge was unusual in that it boasted seven different methods of signalling in the five 'boxes along its length. Normal passenger services had ceased by the 1920s, but considerable traffic was still generated by the Longbridge car plant (for which a workmen's service operated until the 1950s) and the Stewart & Lloyds tube works, close by at Coombs Wood. Freight to Longbridge ceased in 1964 and to Old Hill in 1969.

Two views of Cutnall Green Halt, between Droitwich and Hartlebury, on the line opened by the Oxford, Worcester & Wolverhampton Railway in 1852. By the 1920s bus services had started taking traffic away from the railways, and the GWR responded by opening new stations all over the network to generate traffic. In reality most of these were fairly basic, often built of railway sleepers with perhaps a corrugated-iron waiting shelter. This halt was opened in 1928, when the existing Hampton Lovett signalbox was renamed Cutnall Green. These photographs were taken on Thursday 25 March 1965, just days before services ceased. The signalbox closed in March 1969.

Worcester used to have three suburban stations/halts on the line to Malvern, all of which closed from Monday 5 April 1965. Henwick had opened with the line, but the other two — Boughton Halt and Rushwick Halt — both opened for traffic on 31 March 1924. This is Rushwick Halt in the summer of 1964, with an evening train bound for Bromyard. Just over a track's length in front of '57xx' pannier tank No 4613 is a GWR Automatic Train Control ramp; introduced in 1906, this amazing system could, even then, stop a train automatically if a signal were passed at danger.

*Right:* Leigh Court station in the last summer it was open, 1964. The train is the evening service from Worcester to Bromyard, which left the main line to Malvern and Hereford at Bransford Road Junction (until September 1950 known as Leominster Junction). Leigh Court was the first station on the branch and had opened in 1874. Judging by the rust on the rails the sidings had seen little recent use; by now they were controlled from the ground frame (visible by the telegraph post), which had replaced the signalbox in October 1956.

*Right:* On 3 November 1962 the National Model Railroad Association of America (NMRA) hired a special train, and, for the princely sum of £42, Ellis James-Robertson (see page 64) had arranged with BR that its members could drive and fire the real thing themselves. Collett '2251' 0-6-0 No 2210 is seen running round at Suckley; between here and Bromyard the train made no fewer than 10 journeys. Note the two white flags either side of the headboard — typical American practice on special trains. No 2210 was allocated to Leamington Spa (84D) at this time and survived until June 1965, the final member of its class in BR service.

*Right:* The view east from the road bridge at Fencote station on the occasion of the special last train from Worcester to Leominster and return, hauled by Prairie tank No 4571, on Saturday 26 April 1958. This section between Bromyard and Leominster had closed on 15 September 1952 as part of a campaign to reduce coal consumption nationally, becoming the first Western Region branch to close following the establishment of the Transport Users' Consultative Committee. Fencote was approached by very steep gradients in both directions (1 in 44 and 1 in 46), and as a result the shunting of goods trains here was strictly controlled.

*Above:* To say that, at its end, the passenger service from Bromyard was sparse would be something of an understatement; on most days if you missed the 7.40am train to Worcester the next was not until 5.15pm. In April 1955 the down platform (right) was shortened by 150ft at the Leominster end, clearly visible here with weeds growing on it; having filled up with water from the column in the foreground, the branch tank engine has run round its train and is about to couple back onto the three coaches. The Worcester service continued until September 1964.

*Right:* The view west from the road bridge adjacent to Bromyard station on Saturday 3 November 1962. Bromyard had been connected by rail to Worcester since 1877, although the extension west to Leominster was not completed until 1897. This extension closed to all traffic on 15 September 1952, ostensibly as part of a nationwide campaign to save coal. The track was finally lifted in 1959, just the short section visible here being left to enable locomotives to run round their coaches in the station.

"STEPHENSON LOCOMOTIVE SOCIETY"
(MIDLAND AREA)
SPECIAL LAST TRAIN
from WORCESTER and BROMYARD
to LEOMINSTER
Branch of the former Great Western Rwy
SATURDAY, 26th APRIL 1958
Worcester (Shrub Hill and Foregate Streets
Bromyard, Rowden Mill, Fencote,
Steen's Bridge, Leominster and return
to Worcester (Shrub Hill).
(W) (1266)
For conditions see over

*Above:* The first genuine LMS design emerged from Horwich Works, Lancashire, in 1926. Very successful, this was noticeably different from anything seen previously; most striking was the high running plate over the large cylinders that gave the locomotives their nickname of 'Land Crabs' (later simply 'Crabs'). Designer George Hughes insisted on a low boiler pressure to limit maintenance costs, but achieving the necessary tractive effort meant large cylinders, inclined to stay within the loading gauge. Here No 42827, allocated to Birkenhead (8H), accelerates a train of coke wagons northwards past Leominster South 'box (opened 1875) in September 1964.

*Right:* Viewed from the A44 road bridge, No 1420 takes water at Leominster before working the branch freight to Kington and Presteigne in September 1964. Leominster station is just visible in the background; not visible is its distinctive signalbox, dismantled earlier in the year. The route to Bromyard (closed in 1952) was on the right; the town's bypass now follows a similar path, paralleling the LMS/GW Shrewsbury–Hereford line south of Leominster. A Hereford locomotive at the time of the photograph, No 1420 was withdrawn two months later from Gloucester but survived to pass into preservation, arriving on the Dart Valley Railway in October 1965.

49

No wonder Titley Junction looks to be having an April shower — it's 28 April 1964. By this time a shadow of its former self, it was once the junction for four separate lines. To the east was the line from Leominster, to the west its continuation to Kington and eventually New Radnor, while the line south through Lyonshall and Almeley was one of those taken up during World War 1 and subsequently re-laid, only to shut again, permanently, in 1940. No 1420, however, has arrived from the Presteigne branch to the north, although by this time the physical connection had been moved about a mile to the east.

PREST EIGNE
THE 19 64 END

This location, in deepest rural Herefordshire, is Bullock's Mill, between Kington and Titley Junction. It may seem unbelievable, but from 1820 until 1837 what was then the longest railway in the country — a 36-mile horse-drawn railway all the way from Brecon (although it would nowadays be regarded as a tramway) — ran through here. Making its way back to Leominster on a sunny afternoon in September 1964, having earlier in the day worked the last inbound freight to Presteigne (see rear of coal bunker), is the now-preserved 0-4-2 tank No 1420. The blue Ford Corsair, AWP 828B, was the family car at the time.

Collett '14xx' 0-4-2T No 1420 shunting in the original terminus station at Kington, which became part of the goods yard in 1875, when the extension west to New Radnor was opened. The photograph was taken on Tuesday 28 April 1964, by which time the goods train from Leominster ran on Tuesdays, Thursdays and Saturdays, passenger services having been withdrawn in 1955; on the left are wagons of gas-main pipes to be taken on to Presteigne, served on Tuesdays and Thursdays only. The cost of the return trip in the guard's van was 10s 9d.

NOT TRANSFERABLE.

FORM OF PERMIT FOR TRAVEL IN GUARD'S VAN
OR OTHER NON-PASSENGER CARRYING VEHICLE.

The bearer....................MR. C.N. CLEMENS............................. is
authorised on payment of the appropriate fare to travel on the
...............8.40 a.m................... freight train between
...............LEOMINSTER............... and....KINGTON AND PRESTEIGN & RETURN
in the guard's van or other vehicle not usually provided for
the accommodation of passengers upon and subject to the release
and indemnity signed by the bearer or his employer.

* ~~Available until the end of current half-year from~~

* Available only for use on the .......Tues day of...28/4/..19..64.

The only Welsh location in the book: Presteigne, just over the border, and one-time county town of Radnor. When the Leominster & Kington Railway reached here in 1875 from Titley Junction it spelled the name with no 'e' at the end; clearly there were differing ideas over the years *(inset)*. Passenger services were sparse; in 1947 there were two trains a day (except Sundays) to and from Kington — three on Saturdays — but all were withdrawn in 1951. Freight continued until September 1964, this being the last arrival.

Having arrived with a Worcester–Hereford service, No 6877 *Llanfair Grange* pauses at Great Malvern on Monday 5 November 1962. From here there is a climb of 1 in 80 up to the tunnel through the Malvern Hills. Construction of the Worcester–Hereford line (opened in 1861) was eagerly awaited, this being seen as a means of connecting the Midland Railway to the industries of South Wales via Abergavenny and Pontypool on the standard gauge; the GWR's South Wales main line along the north bank of the River Severn was broad-gauge-only until 1872.

Running light up the 1-in-80 gradient from Great Malvern towards Malvern Wells, Fowler '4MT' tank No 42340 passes the site of Malvern & Tewkesbury Junction in 1958; the signalbox here had closed in November 1954. The line to Upton-on-Severn, Tewkesbury and Ashchurch (closed on 1 December 1952) branched off to the left, where there was also an engine shed and turntable for the branch locomotive. The track towards Upton was recovered in 1958, but a stub was retained for access to the sidings.

*Left:* Viewed from atop the eastern entrance of the 'new' 1,585yd Malvern (Colwall) Tunnel in the summer of 1963, an unidentified Beyer Peacock 'Hymek' Type 3 diesel-hydraulic heads west with train 1T10, the 1.15pm Paddington–Hereford. The 'Hymeks' had only recently been introduced on the route, and this one had probably taken over from steam at Worcester Shrub Hill, leaving there at 4pm. On the left of the picture can be discerned the trackbed leading to the old tunnel, superseded in August 1926.

*Right:* Spring 1965 at Colwall, with one of the few passenger trains still scheduled for steam haulage. 'Large Prairie' No 6129 had worked out from Worcester to Ledbury at about 4.30pm, stopping at all stations and halts along the way. Return from Ledbury was at about 5.45pm, and the locomotive is awaiting departure from Colwall before heading into the single-track tunnel through the Malvern Hills. The '61xx' tanks were designed to work suburban services out of Paddington, and when these were 'dieselised' they were transferred away; by the time of this photograph No 6129 was based at Stourbridge. The entire class was withdrawn by the end of 1965, although one example, No 6106, survives in preservation.

*Left:* No 7031 *Cromwell's Castle* ready to depart Ledbury for Worcester in the late summer of 1962. The Worcester & Hereford Railway, opened in the early 1860s, did at least serve the important intermediate towns of Ledbury and Malvern, albeit at a cost of steep gradients, tunnels and viaducts. No 7031 and its train will soon enter the narrow-bore 1,323yd Ledbury Tunnel, on an adverse gradient of 1 in 80; a banking locomotive was kept at Ledbury to assist heavy freights. After No 7031 was withdrawn in July 1963 the author and his father purchased one of its brass cabside numberplates from Swindon Works.

*Left:* The date is 23 June 1962, and pannier tank No 6424 is pausing at Newent with a Gloucestershire Railway Society special, regular passenger trains having been withdrawn with effect from 13 July 1959. Before the opening in the early 1900s of the Great Western's direct route from Gloucester to Birmingham via Stratford-upon-Avon, Newent was on the main GWR route between the two cities via Ledbury, Malvern, Worcester and Kidderminster. The arch in the platform wall (by the station sign) is where the signalbox used to be; another 'box, originally at Aston Magna in Gloucestershire, was erected opposite the station yard in 1948.

*Left:* Barbers Bridge was on the line between Gloucester and Ledbury, which for part of its length followed the route of the Hereford & Gloucester Canal and was opened in 1885. There was once a passing-loop here, but this was taken out of use as far back as 1898. Latterly the line became something of a rural backwater, and passenger services ceased in 1959, although freight traffic continued until 1964 from the Gloucester end as far as Dymock. Here '64xx' 0-6-0PT No 6424 is seen visiting the truncated route with a Gloucestershire Railway Society special on 23 June 1962.

Collett '2251' 0-6-0 No 2249 prepares to leave Hereford, its then home, for Ross-on-Wye and Gloucester on Thursday 7 March 1963. Opened as a broad-gauge line in the 1850s and converted to standard-gauge in 1869, this route was used by expresses between Bristol and the North West when the Severn Tunnel was closed for engineering work. Passenger trains between Hereford and Gloucester, plus the freight service north of Ross, ceased in autumn 1964.

In Victorian times an undesirably complex network of lines developed around Hereford, completely surrounding the city. During the 1890s all passenger services were concentrated on the station seen here, known originally as Hereford Barr's Court. No 7002 *Devizes Castle* has a drink at the north end of the up platform on Thursday 11 October 1962; note the reversed headboard on the smokebox door. The locomotive represents the final development of the 'Castle' class, being fitted with a double chimney and a high-temperature four-row superheater. Despite receiving these modifications as late as July 1961 it would be withdrawn for scrap in March 1964.

A 'Manor' 4-6-0 heads south over the 97yd Ballingham (Carey) Viaduct on the Hereford–Gloucester line. In less than three miles between Ballingham and Ross-on-Wye the railway crossed the River Wye three times. The GWR route map in the Introduction shows this line coloured dotted red, meaning that locomotives heavier than the blue-rated 'Manors' could traverse it at reduced speed — very useful for diversions. The Hereford–Ross section closed to both freight and passengers with effect from 2 November 1964, after a life of 109 years.

One of the best photographs in the collection — an ex-GWR
2-6-2 (Prairie) tank crossing Backney Bridge with a Hereford–
Gloucester train on a pleasant summer's evening in 1963.
The line between Hereford and Ross-on-Wye must have been
expensive to build; there were three bridges over the River Wye,
plus three tunnels. Today this rather isolated spot near the site of
Backney Halt has been turned into a picnic site complete with
tables and chairs, and, with the piers still standing in silent
testament to generations of railwaymen, it is possible to enjoy the
delightful Herefordshire countryside and remember how things
used to be.

*Above:* Although passenger services at Ross-on-Wye finished in the autumn of 1964 freight from Gloucester continued for a further year. The final inbound freight ran on Friday 29 October 1965; here R. E. (Ellis) James-Robertson, a friend of the author's father, films No 78006 shunting the yard at Ross before it made one last trip down to Lydbrook Junction. The BR Standard Class 2 2-6-0s made ideal branch-line locomotives; their light axle load enabled them to work just about anywhere, and they were easy to maintain. No 78006 was built at Darlington in March 1953 and survived until the end of steam at Gloucester in December 1965.

*Right:* On 2 September 1964, not long before cessation of the passenger services, two Prairie tanks pass at Ross-on-Wye. Running in bunker-first from Hereford is No 4107, whilst already in the station, having arrived from Gloucester, is No 4157, complete with a patch on its water tank; both locomotives would be withdrawn from service in June 1965. Until January 1959 it was possible to change trains here for the scenic route to Symonds Yat and Monmouth that had opened in 1873. The last day upon which it was possible to board a branch passenger train at Ross-on-Wye was Saturday 31 October 1964.

*Left:* The Lydbrook Cable Works (Edison Swan) at Lydbrook Junction, photographed on Friday 29 October 1965. The factory was built in 1912 and during World War 1 produced cable for field telephones; at its height it employed more than 1,200 people. The profusion of cable drums (seen here on the left) was the main reason the branch from Ross-on-Wye was kept open (for freight only) after 1959. These wagons are in the Severn & Wye side of Lydbrook Junction; passenger services from here into the Forest of Dean were discontinued as far back as 1929, and freight in 1956.

*Above:* Lydbrook Junction on Friday 29 October 1965, the date of the final freight train from Ross-on-Wye. BR Standard Class 2 Mogul No 78006, of Gloucester Horton Road shed is standing on the line from Ross, the section on to Monmouth having closed completely in 1959; the cable drums and pallets are from the Lydbrook Cable Works (Edison Swan) — the reason the line between here and Ross stayed open, for freight only. The tracks in the foreground are those of the Severn & Wye Railway (closed 1956), which crossed the 187yd-long Lydbrook Viaduct *en route* to Serridge Junction.

Bilson Junction, near Cinderford in the Forest of Dean, was where trains were assembled before beginning their journey down to Bullo Pill Junction on the Gloucester–South Wales main line. An absolute maze of lines and tramways used to exist in this area, a veritable Clapham Junction in rural Gloucestershire. It was still possible to appreciate its vastness as late as 27 April 1967, not long before complete closure. No D9502 was one of the short-lived Class 14 diesel-hydraulics; the first of an eventual 56 locomotives was completed in July 1964, but BR would withdraw the lot by April 1969.

Whitecroft is between Lydney and Parkend in the Forest of Dean. This view south features Gloucester Horton Road-allocated pannier tank No 6424 standing at the original single platform, opened in 1875 for the commencement of the Severn & Wye Railway passenger service, complete with a typical S&W wooden station building. In 1897 the second platform was added, and the line doubled to Parkend. Regular passenger services had ceased as long ago as 1929; the train shown here was a Gloucestershire Railway Society special, run on 23 June 1962. Thanks to the efforts of the Dean Forest Railway, formed in 1970, trains can once again be seen running through Whitecroft.

*Left:* No 1424 is ready to leave Gloucester Central with an auto-train service up the Golden Valley to Chalford. These Collett 0-4-2 tank engines — updated versions of a design of 1868 — were introduced in 1932, and many would argue that they were the most distinctive and delightful of the GWR's branch line locomotives. No 1424 was allocated to Gloucester for most of its life until withdrawal in December 1963 and attained a mileage of 950,721, the highest for the class.

*Below:* In the early 1900s the GWR introduced a steam railmotor service from Gloucester up the Golden Valley to Chalford, and a number of small halts with lovely-sounding names were opened to encourage traffic. The service was a success and was taken over by push-pull auto-trains. Here one such train from Gloucester calls at Ebley Crossing Halt in the last few weeks of the service. The first stop, nine miles after leaving Gloucester Central, was at Stonehouse (Burdett Road), but in the next seven miles to Chalford there were nine further intermediate stops, this, the first, after 1¼ miles; the next, Cashes Green Halt, was less than ½ mile further on! Collett 0-4-2T No 1453 would be withdrawn upon cessation of the service in November 1964.

*Above:* Seen taking water at Stroud while on an eastbound journey, '14xx' 0-4-2 tank No 1472 entered service in April 1936 and spent much of its life in Wales, around Carmarthen and Newcastle Emlyn, before arriving at Gloucester in May 1961. Withdrawal came in November 1964, when the Golden Valley service ceased. The tickets are dated 7 May 1962 and 27 July 1963.

*Left:* The Chalford auto-train prepares to return downhill to Gloucester, with the driver at the front of the coach and the fireman on the footplate of 0-4-2 tank No 1472. The controls in the coach were connected by mechanical linkage to the locomotive, the advantage of this 'push-pull' operation being there was no need to run round the coach at Gloucester or Chalford. The service ceased on 2 November 1964.

71

*Left:* Kemble, on the WR main line from Gloucester to Swindon, was a junction for the branches to Cirencester (curving away to the right in this view) and Tetbury. The line was built in the 1840s to Brunel's broad gauge of 7ft 0¼in, as evidenced 120 years later by the larger-than-normal gap between the up and down tracks. The station seen here did not open until 1882; previously there were only platforms for people to change trains. Coupled to two auto-coaches, '14xx' 0-4-2 tank No 1472 refills its tanks while on a Gloucestershire Railway Society last-day tour to both Cirencester and Tetbury on Sunday 5 April 1964.

*Left:* A lovely panoramic view of Cirencester Town yard and sidings recorded on Sunday 5 April 1964, the last day of the passenger service. No 1472 is running into the station from Kemble on a special train organised by the Gloucestershire Railway Society. Just to the left of the train is Cirencester locomotive depot, a sub-shed of Gloucester Horton Road. A few hours after this photograph was taken an effigy of Minister of Transport Ernest Marples was burned, despite a leaking gas main! The branch had served the local community for 124 years by the time the freight service finally ceased in 1965.

*Left:* Cirencester Watermoor was on the Midland & South Western Junction Railway (MSWJR), intended as part of a strategic link between Southampton and Birmingham. The GWR already leased a parallel route (the Didcot, Newbury & Southampton), so when the MSWJR became part of the GWR empire in 1923 decline set in. There was a temporary resurgence during World War 2, but by the time of closure to passengers in 1961 there was only one train a day north of Cirencester over the Cotswolds to Cheltenham. This was the scene in 1958; note the fire devil (right), to prevent the water column from freezing.

*Left:* In 1959 Tetbury became the subject of an experiment to improve the economics of rural branches, five lightweight railcars built by AC Cars (the sports-car company) being introduced on the Kemble–Tetbury and Kemble–Cirencester lines. New halts were built to encourage custom, the most famous being Trouble House Halt, which served only the 17th-century Trouble House Inn — presumably in the hope that its customers would travel by train! Passenger traffic increased fivefold, but even this was not enough to save the line, and it closed with effect from 6 April 1964. This was the scene at Tetbury on 26 March — a good drying day?

*Above:* As the diesels took over many steam locomotives were relegated to work out their lives on secondary routes, but the 'Kings', with their heavy (22½-ton) axle loading, had a very restricted route availability, and all had been withdrawn by the end of 1962. No 6018 *King Henry VI* was restored to working order for a final return trip on Sunday 28 April 1963 from Birmingham to its birthplace at Swindon, being seen close by the main GWR locomotive workshops, but was later cut up for scrap.

August Bank Holiday Monday 1961 (when this was at the beginning of the month), with the author in short trousers sitting on the fence. Climbing the Lickey Incline between Bromsgrove and Blackwell with the help of some rear-end assistance is a 'Jubilee', believed to be No 45572 *Erie*. The choice of route north from Cheltenham — eschewing custom by deliberately avoiding centres of population like Tewkesbury, Worcester and Droitwich and then gaining the height necessary to get on to the Birmingham plateau with the worst gradient in the country — has always seemed odd.

*Right:* 'Jubilee' 4-6-0 No 45626 *Seychelles* prepares to climb the Lickey Incline from Bromsgrove to Blackwell — just over two miles at an average gradient of 1 in 37.7 —with an express freight on 1 July 1964. This was the steepest sustained adhesion-worked gradient on BR, and the load was too great for No 45626 to handle on its own; out of sight at the rear was a banking locomotive, Hawksworth 0-6-0PT No 9430. On the far side of the tracks is Rotherham-based 'B1' 4-6-0 No 61372.

*Below right:* The Lickey Incline is one of the most formidable railway gradients in the country. In the steam era virtually every northbound train would need a push, and a dedicated fleet of banking locomotives was maintained at Bromsgrove. Present on the evening of 1 July 1964 were 10 of these Hawksworth-designed pannier tanks, up to four of which would be required to assist a heavy freight; one wonders whether those who settled on the route in the 1830s realised what an operating problem/expense they were inflicting on succeeding generations. Regular steam banking ceased in September 1964.

*Above:* An express freight, with (according to the lamp code on the locomotive) automatic brake operative on at least 50% of the wagons, heads north behind an unidentified Class 9F 2-10-0, the evening sunshine nicely illuminating all those coupled wheels. The date is August 1963, the location east of Norton Junction and north of Abbotswood Junction, where the GWR Worcester–Evesham line passes over the LMS Gloucester–Birmingham route. The '9F' class numbered some 251 locomotives, including *Evening Star*, the very last steam locomotive built by British Railways, turned out by Swindon in March 1960.

*Right:* On their outings together it was generally the author who would take the still photographs while his father made recordings on ciné film, but on this occasion the roles are reversed, and the author can be seen on the platform. Class '9F' 2-10-0 No 92143 entered service in August 1957 and spent its entire career allocated to New England shed (34E) at Peterborough; it was thus a long way from home when photographed heading through Wadborough towards Gloucester. In the era before the closure of so many rural stations in the 1950s and '60s the railway north from here on the direct route to Bromsgrove — a distance of 14 miles 48 chains — was notable for its complete lack of passenger stations.

*Left:* No 6973 *Bricklehampton Hall* northbound between Defford and Wadborough in the summer of 1964, with Bredon Hill just visible on the left; close by is the village of Bricklehampton, the longest solidly written place name in any English-speaking country without a repeating letter! This is the site of Besford station, open only from 1841 to 1846. The fence on the right is the boundary of Defford airfield, where the big radio telescopes are now. From here on 7 June 1942 a Halifax bomber fitted with the prototype secret H2S targeting radar took off and later crashed, killing many of the top researchers in the UK.

*Left:* Class 9F 2-10-0 No 92164 makes a fine sight heading south through Eckington towards Gloucester with an unfitted freight in the summer of 1963. On the far platform, winding up a clockwork ciné camera, is the author's father. The signalbox here was open continuously, controlling the level crossing on Station Road; it was reduced to ground-frame status in 1969, and vehicles now use the bridge in the background.

Two photographs featuring Gloucester-bound trains at Bredon's Norton, between Eckington and Bredon: '8F' No 48606 was recorded on Sunday 1 November 1964, No 4079 *Pendennis Castle*, in charge of a special, a year later. Note the concrete fence posts, just visible in the later picture at the top of the embankment. Apparently the original landowner would only sell on condition that he could shoot rabbits on the embankment; normally fence posts are at the bottom of embankments.

*Left:* Ashchurch Junction signalbox was at the south end of the up platform (*i.e.* from Gloucester). Visible behind it, in this view from early 1958, is the brickwork associated with the new 'box that replaced it in July of that year. The tracks to the right led to Tewkesbury, Upton-on-Severn and (before 1 December 1952) Malvern. At one time there were four signalboxes at Ashchurch, and at the north end of the station until May 1957 there was even a level crossing of two railways — commonplace in the USA but rare in this country.

*Left:* The old Ashchurch Junction signalbox on the up platform looks to be out of use in this view south towards Cheltenham; the new brick-built 'box opposite took over from the old one on 27 July 1958. Ivatt Class 4 2-6-0 No 43013 has just arrived on the 'loop line' from Birmingham via Redditch and Evesham, having run backwards the whole way. These locomotives, introduced in 1947, were bristling with modern features; note the tender with inset coal bunker, to permit improved vision for the enginemen when running backwards.

A summer's evening at Ashchurch in 1963. 'Black Five' No 44776, with 21A (Saltley) shedplate, is homeward-bound on a Gloucester–Birmingham stopping service. The tracks in the foreground, freight-only by this time, are for Tewkesbury. Ashchurch was also junction for the line to Evesham and, before October 1962, Alcester, Redditch and Birmingham; this route avoided the Lickey Incline. This new signalbox, which assumed control of Ashchurch in 1958, would itself close in 1969. In recent years the road bridge has been rebuilt to the north, and a new station — Ashchurch for Tewkesbury — opened, the original having closed in 1971.

*Left:* Having arrived from Birmingham New Street on 20 September 1962, Fowler '4MT' tank No 42417 pauses at Redditch before heading through the 340yd Redditch Tunnel towards Alcester, Evesham and Ashchurch. This service was withdrawn with effect from 1 October 1962 because of the condition of the track north of Evesham, although freight traffic as far as Alcester continued until July 1964. Nowadays the route from Redditch to Birmingham is electrified and sees two trains per hour each way over the single-track section as far as Barnt Green, although Redditch station is now the other side of the road bridge.

*Left:* An Ivatt Class 4 2-6-0 awaits departure for Birmingham from Evesham (Midland) station in September 1962, just before the service was withdrawn. When the track northwards was being removed the demolition train would often be here in the morning when the author's school train arrived at the adjacent GWR station. On one occasion he was allowed to fill the firebox right up with coal before walking the short distance to Prince Henry's Grammar School. During morning assembly the train departed with the safety valves blowing off, covering the school in black smoke and drowning out the headmaster's voice; 'Jack' Miller was not amused, but luckily he never found out the full story!

Evesham (Midland) station as it was in spring 1964. The service through here from Ashchurch to Redditch and Birmingham had ceased from 1 October 1962, due to the poor condition of the track between Evesham and Alcester, although a shuttle service between Evesham and Ashchurch continued until 17 June 1963.

The goods yard is still busy, containing what appear to be some Continental wagons. Access to these tracks was from the still-active GWR station until 1967, when the old Midland Railway yard and sidings were taken out of use.

The appearance at Hinton, on the ex-LMS line between Evesham and Ashchurch, of a 'Castle' on the southbound 'Cornishman' was not a common occurrence but was necessitated early in 1958 by engineering work on the line between Honeybourne and Cheltenham via Broadway and Winchcombe; a new connecting spur was opened between the GWR and LMS lines at Evesham on 15 March 1957 that allowed the diverted trains to travel this way. The presence of the motor cycle under the steps reveals that the signalbox is in use; normally it was open for only about 15 minutes in the afternoon for the weekdays-only freight train to shunt the goods yard.

Hinton, Ashton-under-Hill and Beckford all opened for goods on 1 July 1864 and passengers on 1 October 1864. These three photographs taken at Hinton in May 1964 reveal that it didn't quite make a century. Demolition had started from the Ashchurch end; the contractors were at Beckford in March. Just before the tracks at Hinton vanished forever '2251' 0-6-0 No 2232 disgraced itself by becoming derailed adjacent to the signalbox, and — much to the amusement of local children — No 2291 and the Worcester breakdown train was summoned (via Evesham) to sort out the problem. Within days it had all gone.

The Midland Railway Class 3F 0-6-0s were introduced in 1875. Here, in the summer of 1962, No 43593, allocated to Gloucester Barnwood, is seen heading south through Hinton on the afternoon freight from Evesham to Ashchurch. The line closed completely in 1963, and by May 1964 it was being dismantled; when the author's father visited the site the contractors were about to set fire to the wooden signalbox (seen here in the background), and in exchange for a ten-bob (50p) note he was allowed to take all the signal instruments and 'HINTON' signs.

The train for Tewkesbury and Upton-on-Severn prepares to leave Ashchurch behind ex-Midland Railway '3F' No 43645 in August 1961 (most likely 7 August, as the author has a number of branch tickets stamped with that date; as a treat his father would put young Master Michael on the branch train, asking the guard to keep an eye on him, and then drive to Tewkesbury to collect him!). Passenger services ceased with effect from Monday 14 August, although freight continued to Upton until 1963 and Tewkesbury until 1964.

*Left:* One of the most bizarre classes of locomotive built in the 1930s comprised the 10 LMS '2P' 0-4-4 tank engines, which resurrected a basic design that had last been built new in 1900. The LMS had plenty of boilers that could be recovered from withdrawn engines to keep down the cost (£3,126 per locomotive), and all 10 were completed in just over a month (which included Christmas) at the turn of 1932/3. Pictured in 1958, No 41900, which would end up as the last survivor, approaches Ripple on the afternoon service from Upton-on-Severn to Tewkesbury and Ashchurch.

*Left:* Awaiting departure on the afternoon service to Tewkesbury and Ashchurch, ex-Midland Railway '3F' No 43645 stands at Upton-on-Severn in 1958. Until 1952 the line curving away to the left behind the train continued as far as Malvern. At the time of his death in 1987 the author's father was writing a book on the history of this line, and his research subsequently formed the basis of an article (by David Postle, of Kidderminster Railway Museum) published in the October 2001 issue of *Steam Days* magazine.

Upton-on-Severn on Monday 7 August 1961. By this time the service from Ashchurch and Tewkesbury was very meagre, the train seen at the platform (behind Midland '3F' 0-6-0 No 43645) being the only arrival of the day! The line was singled as early as the 1920s, and from 1 December 1952 the continuation to Malvern was closed; the passenger service from Ashchurch was withdrawn only a week after this photograph was taken, ceasing with effect from 14 August 1961, while freight succumbed on 1 July 1963. Much more custom would surely have been generated if trains between Worcester and Cheltenham had used this route, calling at Malvern, Upton and Tewkesbury — an opportunity lost years ago.

Standish Junction, south of Gloucester, is where the ex-GWR line to Swindon and the ex-LMS line to Bristol diverge. Class 9F 2-10-0 No 92118 was Bristol-bound when photographed in the summer of 1963, with the GWR tracks beyond. These heavy-freight locomotives are generally regarded as the most successful of the classes designed and built by the nationalised British Railways; in service they proved amazingly versatile and even occasionally hauled crack express-passenger trains. No 92118 entered service from Crewe works on 28 December 1956 and would survive almost to the end of main-line steam on BR, being withdrawn from Carnforth, Lancashire, in May 1968.

*Above:* Signalled for the Bristol line, a 'Modified Hall' passes Standish Junction with a partially fitted express freight. The photograph was taken in the last weeks of the Chalford auto-train service, which finished at the beginning of November 1964. Being installed at this time (and visible here in the foreground) was a new connection enabling Paddington–Cheltenham trains to travel direct via Gloucester Eastgate instead of having to reverse at Central station.

*Right:* Stroud (Cheapside) station was 1 mile and 7 chains from the junction station of Dudbridge, on the line from Stonehouse to Nailsworth. The branch had been built in 1885, joining the Midland Railway empire a year later, and at the Grouping became part of the London, Midland & Scottish Railway. Passenger services were withdrawn on 16 June 1947, but freight continued until 1966. The photograph was taken on the occasion of the visit by the Railway Enthusiasts' Club on Saturday 15 April 1956.

*Above:* Coaley Junction on the old Bristol & Gloucester Railway, photographed from a northbound freight in November 1968. On the left is the branch to Cam and Dursley, dating from 1856. The Lister works at Dursley provided much traffic over the years, freight surviving until 1970, whereas the passenger service finished in September 1962. The main line part of Coaley Junction closed at the beginning of 1965 together with most intermediate stations between Bristol and Gloucester. On a more positive note a new station, Cam & Dursley, opened in 1994 slightly to the east of this view.

*Left:* The 2.20pm from Coaley Junction, on the Gloucester–Bristol line, has just arrived at Dursley on Saturday 27 January 1962 behind GWR-designed '74xx' pannier tank No 7435. The branch, 2 miles and 36 chains in length, had a single intermediate station at Cam and was opened in 1856 by the Dursley & Midland Junction Railway. The terminus at Dursley, with just one platform face, was cramped, the run-round loop being outside the station. The Lister Works here generated considerable traffic over the years, freight continuing until July 1970, but the passenger service was withdrawn with effect from 10 September 1962.

*Above:* Sharpness was directly connected by rail to Lydney, on the other side of the River Severn, via the Severn Bridge until 25 October 1960. Late that evening, in thick fog, two barges with a cargo of oil and petrol missed the entrance to Sharpness docks and collided with the railway bridge, demolishing two spans and igniting their load; five people were killed, and the bridge was never repaired. This photograph from the summer of 1963 shows No 1409 — by then the oldest member of the '14xx' class — ready to leave Sharpness on the remaining service to Berkeley Road, which would continue until the autumn of 1964.

*Right:* When diesels started arriving in quantity BR found that so many of the now surplus steam engines needed cutting up that its own workshops couldn't cope, and private contractors were used around the country. This was the scene at Coopers Metals Ltd, California Siding, Sharpness, Gloucestershire, in September 1964, with two 'Castles' close to extinction. Although the class numbered 171 locomotives the design changed over time, and some significant modifications were made in later years up to 1961. Notice the valuable (and not normally visible) copper inner fireboxes, with all the stays connecting to the outer fireboxes; the locomotive nearer the camera had a two-row superheater, the other a four-row.

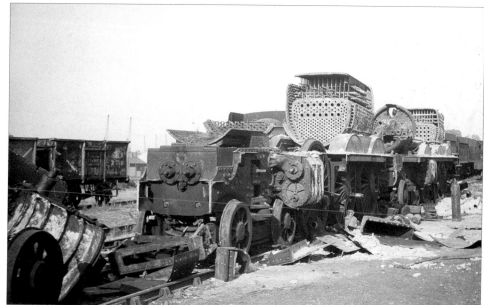

*Right:* Nestling between the Cotswolds and the Mendips is Bath. Seen at the city's Green Park shed (82F) on a wet day in July 1963 is No 53809, one of the famous '7F' 2-8-0s, a type introduced in 1914 by the Somerset & Dorset Joint Railway to haul heavy freight trains over the Mendips. Eventually the class totalled 11 locomotives; the last survivor was withdrawn in September 1964, but two, including No 53809, survive in preservation.

*Below:* The date is Thursday 2 December 1965, and BR Standard Class 5 4-6-0 No 73001 is ready to leave Bath Green Park over the famous Somerset & Dorset route to Bournemouth with the morning through train from Bristol, while at the far platform stands a BR Class 3 2-6-2 tank at the head of a Bristol service. The S&D had been scheduled to close at the end of the month, but due to problems with the provision of replacement bus services the trains continued running until March 1966. The impressive station buildings still survive, Sainsbury's having purchased the site and restored them to something approaching their former glory.